AUGUST IS A THIN GIRL

I0139494

Julie Marie Myatt

BROADWAY PLAY PUBLISHING INC
New York
www.broadwayplaypublishing.com
info@broadwayplaypublishing.com

Cover photo by Julie Marie Myatt
First printing: June 2008
I S B N: 978-0-88145-376-8

Book design: Marie Donovan
Word processing: Microsoft Word
Typographic controls: Ventura Publisher
Typeface: Palatino
Printed and bound in the U S A

CHARACTERS & SETTING

EVE, *early thirties*
GEORGE, *mid to late thirties*
MANAGER, *forties, Korean*
LILY, *ten years old* (EVE *as a young child*)
DEAN, *teenager, Korean*
BELINDA, *early twenties*

Place: Idaho. Off the highway. A run-down motel.

Time: Present

ACT ONE

Scene One

(A motel room. Night)

(The key rattles as EVE *enters through the door and automatically locks it behind her. Looks around the dark room for a light. She finds a lamp by the bed.)*

*(*EVE*, and the room, look better in the dark.)*

*(*EVE *is too thin and road dirty. Thirty-two but looks much younger—the arrested development of a young girl. She has a nervous laugh.)*

(It's a cheap motel room with unmatching furniture and a tattered blanket on the bed. A bad landscape painting hangs above it.)

*(*EVE *turns on the air conditioner but it doesn't work. She takes off her clothes, suddenly too hot in her jeans and T-shirt. Keeps her underwear and tank top on.)*

*(*EVE *picks up the ice bucket and heads for the door. She unlocks it, opens it, and remembers she's not dressed. She throws on her jeans. Runs out the door, and reappears with ice.)*

*(*EVE *closes the door behind her and locks it again. Double checking to make sure it is indeed, locked.)*

*(*EVE *strips off her jeans again. Begins to unwrap a plastic cup when there's a knock on the door. She panics.)*

*(*EVE *puts on her jeans.)*

EVE: Who is it? *(She stands by the door.)* Who is it?

MANAGER: *(O S)* Manager.

(EVE unlocks it.)

(The MANAGER stands with a slip of paper in hand.)

MANAGER: Your card was declined.

EVE: What?

MANAGER: Your credit card. Declined.

EVE: Oh no...really?

MANAGER: Really. I can't let you stay if you don't pay—

EVE: Just a second. *(She fishes through her pockets. She finds three dollars. She searches through one of her bags and finally pulls out a twenty.)* Here.

MANAGER: It's twenty-one ninety-nine. June through August.

(EVE hands two of the bills to the MANAGER.)

MANAGER: Check out's at noon.

EVE: Sorry about the card. I just sent a payment yesterday, I guess it didn't clear—

(The MANAGER shuts the door.)

(EVE holds the dollar in her hand, then puts it in her pocket before she takes off her pants. Again. She takes off her tank top and stares at herself in the mirror. She examines her flat stomach, as if it's new.)

(A knock)

(EVE quickly dresses and unlocks the door.)

EVE: You can't decline cash—

(GEORGE stands outside the door. Late twenties. Tall. And would be considered gawky and awkward if he weren't so confident. Cocky.)

GEORGE: I can't?

EVE: You've got the wrong room.

GEORGE: Do you know Belinda?

EVE: No.

GEORGE: She said this was her room. 29.

EVE: This is 25.

GEORGE: Oh yeah...look at that.

EVE: Try down there.

GEORGE: Why?

EVE: I think the rooms get higher. That way.

GEORGE: Maybe I'd rather stay here.

(EVE slams and locks the door. GEORGE leans up against it.)

GEORGE: You're much prettier than Belinda.

(EVE leans against the other side.)

EVE: Go away please.

GEORGE: Why?

EVE: Please?

GEORGE: I didn't mean to scare you.

EVE: Just go.

GEORGE: I'm sorry.

EVE: Go find your girlfriend.

GEORGE: She's not my girlfriend.

EVE: Go.

GEORGE: Why?

EVE: Please.

GEORGE: Why?

EVE: Just—please? I'm not feeling...

(GEORGE *listens.*)

GEORGE: I'm sorry. *(He exits.)*

(EVE *listens.*)

(EVE *passes the mirror and goes into a seizure. She hits her head on a table and hits the floor, writhes and twists as the stage goes dark.)*

(Slides of perfect houses flash against the wall of the stage. LILY, a ten year old girl, enters carrying glue and a hammer and keys in one hand, crayons and a box of Barbies in the other. The slides continue against the wall and LILY's body as she looks in front and behind her, in the distance and beyond the audience.)

(The slides progress, more houses, and then windows inside the houses. The slides change to living rooms. Kitchens. Furniture. Couches. Chairs. Beds. As the slides flash on the wall, LILY is inside the houses, amongst the furnishings, but still searching. Sometimes there are people in the slides with her, sometimes she is the only one in the room.)

(The slides change to windows that look out on yards. Then flash to back yards and LILY is standing in the yards with swings and patio furniture. Picnic tables. Some have bikes and children in the yards, some have dogs.)

(Still searching, LILY walks off stage. Leaving the slides and the happy yards behind.)

(The slides end.)

(EVE *blinks. And slowly comes to.)*

Scene Two

(The T V is the only light in the room. EVE *sits droned by the sound. A commercial for a collection of love songs plays.)*

(A knock)

(Another knock)

EVE: Who is it?

GEORGE: What?

*(*EVE *moves closer to the door.* GEORGE *can be seen on the other side.)*

EVE: Who is it?

GEORGE: George.

EVE: Who?

GEORGE: The guy that scared you.

EVE: Uh...you, you didn't scare me.

GEORGE: Then open the door.

EVE: No.

GEORGE: Why not?

EVE: I don't know you.

GEORGE: We just met an hour ago.

EVE: What about Melinda? Belinda? *(She dresses.)*

GEORGE: Will you please open the door?

EVE: No.

GEORGE: Why not?

EVE: It's my room.

GEORGE: I'm not going to hurt you.

EVE: I don't feel like company. (*She shuts off the television.*)

GEORGE: Just open the door.

EVE: Please go away.

GEORGE: Why?

EVE: I want to be alone. How many ways do I have to say it?

GEORGE: Until you believe it, I guess.

(EVE *unlocks the door.*)

EVE: Fuck you.

(GEORGE *holds/offers a six pack of beer and a bag of sandwiches.*)

EVE: What happened to Belinda?

GEORGE: There was a big fat man in her room.

EVE: She ditched you.

GEORGE: Her husband.

EVE: What's in the bag?

GEORGE: A gun.

EVE: That's not funny. (*She tries to close the door.*)

GEORGE: I'm sorry. You just look so scared, I can't help it. (*He steps inside.*) I always wondered what these rooms were like. Much less than I expected...much less. But...I guess you were lucky to get anything. This time of year. August is our busiest month, you know.

(EVE *remains by the door.*)

EVE: Uh huh, well—

GEORGE: Everyone's rushing to get their vacation. Moving someplace—

EVE: I'm just passing through—

GEORGE: I brought you dinner.

EVE: I really wasn't planning to stop—

GEORGE: I made it myself.

(EVE *closes the door.*)

EVE: Oh.

GEORGE: What happened to your eye?

EVE: Nothing. I fell.

(EVE *moves to another side of the room. And for the rest of the scene, she and* GEORGE *pace to different areas of the room. Never sitting on the bed, but occasionally touching it as they pass each other.*)

GEORGE: Huh.

EVE: Tripped.

GEORGE: Huh.

(GEORGE *picks up* EVE's *keys. She watches him carefully with her keys.*)

GEORGE: You get too tired to drive any farther and stop here?

EVE: Yeah.

GEORGE: The whole place counts on that. (*He sets the keys down.*)

EVE: Desperation?

GEORGE: Pretty much. We're here to serve you. Fill it. Pump it. Fix it. Clean off the bugs. Check it. Check it again. Fix it again. Or kick it, if that's all you want. See? (*He holds up his greasy hands.*)

EVE: Which station?

GEORGE: The one by the highway.

EVE: I saw—

GEORGE: My dad's. Hap's.

EVE: The Chevron?

GEORGE: Best service and cleanest restrooms in town.

(GEORGE *hands* EVE *a ballpoint pen.*)

GEORGE: Free pen with every fill up.

(EVE *takes the pen and reads the side.*)

EVE: I stopped there. To use the phone. I didn't see you.

GEORGE: No?

EVE: No.

GEORGE: I must have been under a car or something—
It's hot in here.

EVE: The air conditioner's broken.

(GEORGE *lifts up the panel on the air conditioner and fixes it.
It comes on with a loud hum.*)

(EVE *shuts it off.*)

EVE: Thanks.

GEORGE: It's not healthy.

EVE: It's too loud.

GEORGE: Loud?

EVE: It's my room. (*She stares out the window.*)

GEORGE: You want a beer?

(EVE *doesn't respond.*)

GEORGE: Beer? (*He holds it out to her.*) You don't like this
kind?

EVE: Kind what?

GEORGE: Beer?

EVE: Michelob?

GEORGE: Looks like you're used to more expensive stuff.

EVE: Me?

GEORGE: Yeah.

EVE: Right.

GEORGE: Fancy girl.

EVE: No...

GEORGE: It's written all over you.

EVE: Is it? *(She looks herself over. Searching)*

GEORGE: Your shoes.

EVE: I'm not wearing any.

GEORGE: Over there.

EVE: They weren't expensive.

GEORGE: Still...it's obvious you've been other places than here.

EVE: I'm in a motel.

GEORGE: Other, *other* places.

EVE: Have you been other, *other* places?

GEORGE: Do I look like it?

(EVE takes the beer. Looks him over)

EVE: Maybe other places are overrated.

GEORGE: I wouldn't know.

EVE: Misleading.

GEORGE: I wouldn't know—

EVE: Ever been in a dark forest?

GEORGE: No.

EVE: Huh.

GEORGE: Sounds like Dorothy.

EVE: Dorothy? Oh right...Oz.

GEORGE: Yeah.

EVE: That was a dream.

GEORGE: So is Idaho. Don't you read the billboards?

EVE: Maybe.

GEORGE: Turkey or ham?

EVE: What?

GEORGE: Sandwich.

(GEORGE *hands her the food, as he and* EVE *sit staring at each other. She takes a bite and puts aside the sandwich.*)

GEORGE: You don't like ham?

EVE: I like ham. (*She fades into staring at the floor.*)

GEORGE: You're not very talkative, are you?

EVE: I think I told you I wasn't in the mood for company.

GEORGE: Where are you going?

EVE: What do you mean?

GEORGE: Where are you headed? From here.

EVE: Can I have another beer?

GEORGE: Fast drinker, huh?

EVE: When I'm thirsty.

GEORGE: It's too hot in here. (*He reaches and turns on the air conditioner.*)

EVE: Listen, I'm sorry. Uh...

GEORGE: George.

EVE: George. (*She turns off the air conditioner.*) I hope you're not looking for stimulating conversation. I've had a long day...I drove all the way from Bend—

GEORGE: Oregon?

EVE: Yeah.

GEORGE: Nice.

EVE: Ever been there?

GEORGE: No.

EVE: You've never done that drive? From here?

GEORGE: No.

EVE: Highway twelve, the old Lewis and Clark Trail?

GEORGE: Doesn't ring a bell—

EVE: I saw a moose.

GEORGE: Sure.

EVE: She ran in front of my car. I saw her breathing—

GEORGE: Lewis and Clark...oh yeah...I know those guys. They're pretty popular around here—

(EVE *takes a large drink.*)

EVE: I peed my pants.

GEORGE: Really?

(EVE *laughs. She fishes a quarter from her pocket, looks at it, puts it back.*)

GEORGE: What were you doing there?

EVE: Where?

GEORGE: Bend.

EVE: Oh. Bend.

GEORGE: Yeah.

EVE: Have you been there? ...Right. No. Sorry—

GEORGE: Going around it?

EVE: Sleeping.

GEORGE: Sleeping. Alone?

EVE: Why?

GEORGE: Why not?

EVE: Trying to sleep.

GEORGE: Alone?

(They both take a drink. EVE takes a few steps farther from GEORGE.)

GEORGE: What's your name?

EVE: What?

GEORGE: I don't know your name.

(GEORGE moves closer to EVE.)

EVE: Oh. You don't.

GEORGE: No.

EVE: Huh.

GEORGE: What is it?

EVE: Oh.

(GEORGE waits.)

EVE: Eve.

(GEORGE holds out his hand. Smiles. Moves closer. EVE takes a drink of beer, unaware.)

GEORGE: Are you always so distracted?

EVE: What?

GEORGE: Where are you from?

(EVE keeps drinking.)

GEORGE: So, Eve, where are you from?

(EVE just looks at GEORGE.)

GEORGE: Let me guess...I'm usually pretty good at this. New York?

(EVE *leans on a chair.*)

GEORGE: Las Vegas?

EVE: No where.

GEORGE: C'mon. Everyone's from somewhere... unless you're trying to be mysterious.

EVE: I've moved alot.

GEORGE: Circus?

EVE: Yes.

GEORGE: Really?

EVE: Tight rope walker.

GEORGE: Really?

(EVE *laughs.*)

GEORGE: Crime?

EVE: Yes.

GEORGE: Really?

EVE: Rope thief.

GEORGE: Really?

EVE: My dad was a Marine.

GEORGE: Right.

EVE: Really.

GEORGE: Sergeant?

EVE: No.

GEORGE: Major?

EVE: General.

GEORGE: Uh huh.

EVE: Really.

GEORGE: Whoa...The General's Daughter. Sleeping in Idaho.

EVE: Trying. *(She stretches her arms. Rubs her face. Looks out the window)*

GEORGE: Did he make you salute?

EVE: Who?

GEORGE: Your Dad.

EVE: Oh. No.

GEORGE: Did he make you march?

EVE: No.

GEORGE: Stand at attention?

EVE: Always.

(GEORGE takes a drink.)

GEORGE: Wow.

EVE: Yeah.

GEORGE: Did you like it?

EVE: What?

GEORGE: All that moving.

EVE: Not particularly.

GEORGE: Looks like you're still doing it.

EVE: Uh huh.

GEORGE: Where're you going again?

(EVE sits in a chair.)

(GEORGE waits for a response.)

GEORGE: Where're are you—

EVE: I'm really not in the mood to talk.

GEORGE: Have you thought about it?

EVE: What?

GEORGE: Staying some place.

EVE: Where?

GEORGE: Anywhere.

EVE: Of course. I've thought about it.

GEORGE: Where?

EVE: Everybody thinks about it.

GEORGE: Where?

EVE: I had to think about something.

GEORGE: No. I mean now. Pulling off someplace—

EVE: Stuck in the back seat with my sister—

GEORGE: Turning off the engine—

EVE: Staring out the window—

GEORGE: Staying—

EVE: My eyes would ache at night...

GEORGE: You could break down—

EVE: I'd watch the rain drops race down the glass—

GEORGE: You know. Stop—

EVE: Or farmers plowing crops, kids riding bikes with fishing poles—

GEORGE: I fish—

EVE: Our eyes would meet...I'd hide my envy—

GEORGE: Where did you live the longest—

EVE: And wave instead. Do you ever wave to people?

GEORGE: What?

EVE: When they pass by?

GEORGE: What?

EVE: Wave.

GEORGE: Sure—

EVE: How do you do it?

GEORGE: What?

EVE: Wave.

GEORGE: What?

EVE: Do you hold up your hand like this? (*She demonstrates. A kind of good-bye wave*) Or more like this? (*She demonstrates. A kind of hello wave*)

GEORGE: What?

EVE: Which one? (GEORGE *does a wave that's somewhere in between good-bye and hello.*)

EVE: Huh.

GEORGE: Why? How about you?

EVE: I'd rather nod. (*She demonstrates. Looks a trucker passing another trucker*)

GEORGE: What does that mean?

EVE: I'm not sure. (*She smiles. Laughs*)

GEORGE: Why do you do it?

EVE: My hands are tired.

GEORGE: So where's home?

EVE: Must we talk?

GEORGE: No. No. We can—

(GEORGE *moves toward* EVE—)

EVE: Can't we just sit here?

GEORGE: Sure. (*He quickly sits on the dresser.*) It's hot in here.

(EVE *closes her eyes.* GEORGE *watches her.*)

GEORGE: Where's the General live?

EVE: Why?

GEORGE: I've never met a General before.

EVE: He's retired.

GEORGE: Oh. Where's he live?

(EVE *looks at* GEORGE.)

EVE: Why? You want to bring him a sandwich?

GEORGE: Maybe.

EVE: He's overseas—

GEORGE: Is that home—

EVE: No.

GEORGE: Is your Mom—

EVE: They're getting a divorce.

(GEORGE *watches* EVE *finish off her beer. Tear the label from the bottle*)

(EVE *stops what she's doing and pushes a smile at* GEORGE. *Laughs*)

(EVE *returns to the bottle.*)

GEORGE: You always travel alone?

EVE: What?

GEORGE: You always travel alone?

EVE: I am really not in the mood to talk.

GEORGE: What are you in the mood to do?

EVE: Be alone.

GEORGE: It's not a difficult question.

EVE: For who?

(EVE *reaches in her bag and pulls out a tube of lip balm.*
GEORGE *watches her seem to take forever to apply it to
her lips.*)

EVE: No...I don't. Not always.

GEORGE: Men?

EVE: What's it matter?

GEORGE: Anyone else?

EVE: I had a dog.

GEORGE: What kind? A poodle or something?

EVE: Do I look like I'd own a poodle? (*She glances in
the mirror and walks away.*)

GEORGE: Colonel Sanders' daughter.

EVE: General—

GEORGE: Fancy girl—

EVE: I look real fancy right now, don't I.

GEORGE: You're pretty. Very pretty.

EVE: Liar.

GEORGE: Eve...do I look like a liar?

EVE: Yes.

GEORGE: What does a liar look like?

EVE: The mirror's right there.

GEORGE: So.

EVE: Take a look.

GEORGE: No.

EVE: It's right there.

GEORGE: No thanks.

EVE: Why not?

GEORGE: I don't want to.

EVE: Why not?

GEORGE: 'I'm not in the mood'.

EVE: Why not?

GEORGE: I prefer not to.

EVE: You see ghosts?

GEORGE: No.

EVE: Visions?

GEORGE: No.

EVE: Strangers?

GEORGE: I wouldn't know.

EVE: Why not?

GEORGE: I've never looked.

EVE: Right...

GEORGE: It's true.

EVE: No. Seriously. Go ahead. Take a look. I've tried it.
Makes you look ten pounds lighter. *(She laughs.)*

GEORGE: I'll pass.

EVE: Are you afraid?

GEORGE: No.

EVE: You've never seen yourself.

GEORGE: I've never seen my reflection.

EVE: You have no idea what you look like?

GEORGE: No.

EVE: Wow...

GEORGE: But you can tell me I'm handsome if you want.

EVE: What do you think you look like?

GEORGE: I'd rather talk about your dog.

EVE: Can't.

GEORGE: He run away?

EVE: Yeah.

GEORGE: You ever pick up hitch hikers?

EVE: Sometimes.

GEORGE: Really, we hear stories, at the station. Awful things. You really gotta be careful—

EVE: The last girl had just given away her son.

GEORGE: What?

EVE: She gave her two year old son to another family.

GEORGE: Why—

EVE: Now *she* was pretty. One of those slender—

GEORGE: What?

EVE: One of those girls that barely touch the ground when they walk...ever met those types?

GEORGE: Girls are pretty solid around here—

EVE: Tree fairies—

GEORGE: And she gave up her kid?

EVE: Her car ran out of gas. She was smiling.

GEORGE: And you picked her up?

EVE: Just fifteen minutes with her, and I felt like the Flintstones at the drive-in with that big rack of ribs—

GEORGE: I still laugh when I see that—

EVE: But those girls. Pain doesn't touch them... it doesn't. They are so thin it passes through. There's no room. Everything just floats through...turns to air.

GEORGE: You shouldn't pick up strangers.

EVE: I let you in.

GEORGE: We've met before.

EVE: You could be dangerous.

GEORGE: So could you.

(EVE *begins to go into another seizure. Not as severe as the* *last. She sits blank and unreachable, vacantly staring.)*

GEORGE: Eve?

(LILY *rides a bike on stage, searching something, with a small* *back pack, loaded with toys and things, on her back. A tiny* *American flag is sewn on the pack.)*

(Travel slides of China, India, Japan; then more slides of *Europe: France, England, Italy, Norway...begin on the walls,* *on* GEORGE *and* EVE, *and on* LILY.)

GEORGE: Eve?

(The slides move fast and furious and LILY *is overwhelmed* *by the sights both on her and the walls around her.)*

(LILY *tries to stop the bike, but can't. She must keep riding* *off stage.)*

(EVE *comes to, finally making eye contact. She sits.* GEORGE *huddles beside her on the floor.)*

GEORGE: Are you O K?

EVE: Yeah...

GEORGE: Are you sure? Should I call doctor?

EVE: No.

GEORGE: Are you sure—

EVE: Let, let me just sit here for a minute.

GEORGE: What happened?

EVE: Could we please not—I can't talk right now.

GEORGE: Do you want to be alone?

EVE: No.

Scene Three

(The T V is the only light in the room. The sound is off.)

(EVE sits on the bed.)

(GEORGE still sits on the floor. He's looking up at EVE.)

GEORGE: What's that scar?

EVE: What?

GEORGE: Underneath your chin.

(EVE rubs her chin.)

GEORGE: Can I touch it?

(GEORGE gets up and sits beside EVE.)

EVE: No.

GEORGE: I want to.

EVE: I cut it open three times.

GEORGE: How?

EVE: Once on some cement stairs in Maryland, once while playing with my sister on the floor, also in Maryland, and once on some ice in, in a—

GEORGE: You'd think you'd learn to put your hands in front of you. *(He reaches out to touch the scar—)*

(EVE pulls away.)

EVE: You'd think.

GEORGE: See my arm.

EVE: Are you showing off your muscles?

GEORGE: Yes. See that scar?

EVE: Uh huh.

GEORGE: I fell off my uncle's truck when I was four.
I thought I could fly. My father told the doctor that's
what happens to idiots.

EVE: See my lips.

GEORGE: Yes.

EVE: Underneath them?

GEORGE: Uh huh—

EVE: My dad was pushing my sister and I on some
swings, right after he got home. And my sister asked
him to push her higher. So he pushed both of us higher.
And I let go, flew out of the swing, and bit through my
lip.

GEORGE: You should have held on.

EVE: He felt horrible.

GEORGE: See my lips?

EVE: No.

GEORGE: Maybe you should move closer.

EVE: Why?

GEORGE: You could see where my father pushed me.

EVE: Where?

GEORGE: Into a wall.

(GEORGE *moves in to kiss* EVE—)

EVE: See my eyes.

GEORGE: Are you showing off your eyes?

EVE: No.

GEORGE: You could if you wanted to.

EVE: I'm not.

GEORGE: I don't believe you.

EVE: They're uneven. One works better than the other.

GEORGE: Which one?

EVE: This one.

GEORGE: How do I look?

EVE: I don't know. I need glasses. How do you think you look?

GEORGE: See my nose?

EVE: Yes.

GEORGE: It turns off to the side.

EVE: How do you know? You've never seen it.

GEORGE: I can feel it. Fourth grade fight. A fifth grader called me Georgie Porgie. Would have been O K if he hadn't added the Pudding and Pie. But both nostrils still work the same.

EVE: How do I smell?

GEORGE: Scared.

EVE: Still?

GEORGE: Yeah.

EVE: I guess I haven't showered in awhile. My hands are dirty.

GEORGE: Mine are dirtier.

(GEORGE *tries to touch* EVE's *hand.*)

EVE: See this foot. This foot, this very foot, has walked on the Great Wall of China. Trekked across goat shit in the Himalayas. Dipped in the clear waters of the Mediterranean, just off the coast of France.

GEORGE: What about the other one?

EVE: Well, this one has been kissed by the lips of a loving Japanese man...from Hiroshima of all places. It has been stung by jellyfish in the Atlantic. And it has pushed the peddle to drive across this great land at least five times.

GEORGE: Are you bragging?

EVE: No.

GEORGE: I don't believe you.

EVE: They're just facts. Different from yours.

GEORGE: I'll never know, will I?

EVE: You aren't that old.

GEORGE: I'm not going anywhere.

EVE: You could.

GEORGE: Oh yeah. That's right, I could. Thanks. I forgot. You're the expert. The traveling wonder girl.

EVE: I should just keep my mouth shut. Let everyone else do the talking. I should know that—

GEORGE: What?

EVE: Most people would rather to talk than hear someone else's—

GEORGE: They're just stamps to you.

EVE: What?

GEORGE: Those things, those places—

EVE: You don't know me.

GEORGE: I don't think it matters if your feet have been on the moon and back, it's obvious all you really want is to curl up and be safe. Be taken care of.

EVE: Bullshit—

(EVE *jumps out of bed, away from* GEORGE.)

GEORGE: By someone. Somewhere.

EVE: Bullshit.

GEORGE: Stop for awhile.

EVE: I should keep my mouth shut.

GEORGE: How much money do you have?

EVE: I should know better...always better to listen than talk—

GEORGE: Where are you going?

EVE: None of your business—

GEORGE: Why'd you call your parents?

EVE: What?

GEORGE: I could travel the world too if my parents would send me money when I cried hard enough.

EVE: Fuck you.

GEORGE: Bail me out of strange towns—

EVE: No one's bailing me out.

GEORGE: Dirty motel rooms—

EVE: Fuck you. They don't know where I am.

GEORGE: Then who'd you call?

EVE: Get out.

GEORGE: What's wrong with you?

EVE: I don't have to tell you anything.

GEORGE: You wanna get married?

Scene Four

(Outside the motel room door. GEORGE *rubs his fingers on the metal numbers.)*

(The motel sign flashing in the background.)

*(*EVE *sits on the other side of the door.)*

GEORGE: Eve? ...Eve... Evening. Good Evening. New Year's Eve. Adam and Eve...Christmas Eve. On the Eve of our discontent...I bet you get all those, don't you? ...I didn't mean to make you angry... *(He listens.)* Really. I don't know anything about love. Nothing.

*(*EVE *listens.)*

GEORGE: I just couldn't sit and watch you drive out of town and not try and meet you...

*(*EVE *opens another beer.)*

GEORGE: I mean, it's not every day a guy gets hit with his future.

EVE: I'm not your future.

GEORGE: What?

EVE: I said, I'm not your future.

GEORGE: How do you know?

EVE: You shouldn't need to follow your future.

GEORGE: *Follow* sounds unflattering—I *noticed* you were checking in to this particular motel.

EVE: You *follow* me to my motel room, make up some Belinda girl—

GEORGE: No.

EVE: No what?

GEORGE: I didn't make up Belinda.

EVE: You ask every girl that falls through town to marry you?

GEORGE: No.

EVE: Then why'd you ask me?

GEORGE: I felt like it.

EVE: Can't you find a nice girl here?

GEORGE: I don't want a nice girl here.

EVE: Why not?

GEORGE: I know them all.

EVE: You want a lost girl? *(She laughs.)*

GEORGE: Yes.

EVE: You're full of shit.

GEORGE: Sometimes.

EVE: Really. I think you're a little off.

GEORGE: What do you mean?

EVE: Touched.

GEORGE: Better than lost.

EVE: Why won't you look in the mirror?

GEORGE: Why should I?

EVE: To see who you are.

GEORGE: I already know.

EVE: I look in the mirror at least twenty times a day. Maybe more.

GEORGE: You have to see yourself to believe it?

EVE: Sometimes.

GEORGE: So what do you look like?

EVE: I don't know— *(She laughs.)*

GEORGE: After seeing yourself so many times?

(EVE rubs a bruise on her arm.)

EVE: Something pale blue.

GEORGE: What?

EVE: Pale blue—

GEORGE: What's that—

EVE: With clouds floating through like my arms. My hands. My legs. My chest. And then a breeze will come and show my hair...softer than branches... *(She looks at her dirty hair in her hand.)* I move in closer, my face just touching the glass, and I see a bird, sitting in a rusty cage...with a small red chest...panting...and I know that somewhere in there, I do exist...the pieces of me are floating and changing around in the blue...but I will put them together. *(She curls up her legs to her chest.)* Eventually.

GEORGE: Sounds horrible.

EVE: Maybe no more horrible than trying to put together a car.

GEORGE: A car can't feel pain.

EVE: No.

GEORGE: And it can't curl up next to another car—

EVE: Maybe that's what car accidents are for.

GEORGE: Can I come back inside?

EVE: No.

GEORGE: Are you still afraid of me?

EVE: Yes.

GEORGE: Why?

EVE: I don't know you.

GEORGE: I'm George. We've met—

EVE: Tell me what you look like.

GEORGE: Why does it matter? Can't you trust what you think I look like? Who you think I am?

EVE: I want to hear it from you.

GEORGE: Why?

EVE: I want to know if I recognize you before I let you in, don't I? *(She laughs.)*

(GEORGE sits down on the other side of the door. They sit back to back, only the wood between them.)

GEORGE: I think...I think maybe I am the color brown. Or how you feel when you look at the color brown. Maybe.

EVE: Brown?

GEORGE: Yeah. When I was a kid, I think, I think, I used to feel kind of orange. Just felt orange all the time and that when people saw me, they felt like they did when they looked at the color orange. Kind of put off at first, but then they liked how much fun I could be and how bright I was in the back yard. But now...

EVE: Now...

GEORGE: I've changed. I am not that bright color anymore, but something more dull. Tired. And yet, not bad, but just not a burst of color. Comfortable to some. Boring to others. Earth and Idaho kid. Brown.

EVE: And is that good?

GEORGE: It's just what it is. Like brown. It may seem like dirt or just plain shit, but it's what it is. Nothing more. And maybe only less if you wanted red or yellow instead.

EVE: I see. *(She is beginning to fall asleep.)*

GEORGE: What color do you want?

EVE: Hmm...

GEORGE: Is brown enough for a fancy girl?

(EVE is finally asleep.)

Scene Five

(A sing-song knock on the door.)

EVE: George?

(EVE unlocks and opens the door. DEAN, a sixteen year old kid, stands on the other side with a plunger.)

DEAN: Backed up, huh?

EVE: No.

DEAN: My father said there was a back up in 29.

EVE: This is 25.

DEAN: Oh yeah...how's yours?

EVE: My what?

DEAN: Toilet.

EVE: Fine.

DEAN: There's been some trouble in this room before. Two A M is nothing for me. It happens all the time.

EVE: Was there a guy out here?

DEAN: What kind of guy?

EVE: Tall. Brownish.

(DEAN is suddenly excited. Whispers)

DEAN: You're a hooker?

EVE: No. *(She laughs.)*

DEAN: Did he beat you up?

EVE: No.

DEAN: You're a prostitute? In those clothes?

EVE: No.

DEAN: My Dad will make you leave. Honest. He said
he saw enough of that kind of thing in Korea. He kicked
two girls out—

EVE: I'm not a prostitute.

DEAN: Are you sure?

EVE: Positive.

DEAN: You can make a lot of money that way.

EVE: I'm sure—

DEAN: If you're into that, you can buy some nice clothes
and shoes and stuff. A new car.

EVE: I'm not—

DEAN: These last two girls, they were real tall and
skinny. Very Pretty. They were from, from Las Vegas,
and, and they had a brand new Mercades. Took me
for a ride in it.

EVE: Really?

DEAN: Before my Dad found them in Room 22 with
four kids from my high school. I felt sorry for them.
They were cool. Gave me a blow job for free.

EVE: Really?

DEAN: It was no big deal. They were only two years
older than me.

EVE: Uh huh.

DEAN: I didn't even have to ask.

EVE: Nice girls.

DEAN: I've seen some things here, you know...but it's all just training, you know. For my big trip.

EVE: Big trip?

DEAN: Home.

EVE: But don't you live here?

DEAN: I was born in Korea. I'm going back.

EVE: Good for you.

DEAN: I'm gonna start in Korea, see my relatives, and then go from there...you know...bounce around the world.

EVE: Sounds like a plan. *(She laughs.)*

DEAN: I'm not rotting in this town like the rest of my friends. I wanna go back to where I was born, you know. I don't remember what it looks like. So I want to go back.

EVE: I've been there.

DEAN: No...? Really?

EVE: My parents used to live there, a few years ago... my dad is there on business now—

DEAN: What's it like?

EVE: Well, it's it's interesting. Busy. *(She laughs.)*

DEAN: I like busy. I'll fit right in. It's weird 'cause I'm from there but I don't remember anything so they'll have to show me everything again. My homeland. I mean, I don't even speak Korean that well, but I was born there. Isn't the weird?

EVE: Listen, I'm tired—

DEAN: Oh, yeah...cool. I understand. Wow...you've been to Korea?

EVE: Yep.

DEAN: I'll be there in two years.

EVE: Say hello to my father, will you?

DEAN: Yeah...sure.

EVE: Thanks.

DEAN: What's his name?

EVE: Homewrecker.

DEAN: Mister Homewrecker?

EVE: Right.

DEAN: Cool.

(EVE *closes the door. She picks up the beer bottles and throws them in the trash by the mirror. She tries not to look at it, even turns away from it. But still it pulls her...to face the mirror. She looks closer. The bruise is getting darker under her eye.)*

Scene Six

(EVE *sits in bed watching television and jumps up as a tipsy* BELINDA *enters and turns on the light.)*

BELINDA: What are you doing in my bed?

EVE: This is my bed.

(BELINDA *shuts off the T V.)*

BELINDA: It's my bed, Goldie Locks. Get out.

(EVE *laughs.)*

EVE: I don't think so—

BELINDA: What room is this?

EVE: 25.

BELINDA: 29?

EVE: Twenty-five.

BELINDA: Damn...I thought that ice machine was farther. Shit.

EVE: Your key opened my room?

BELINDA: Yeah.

EVE: Why?

BELINDA: I've got all the keys.

EVE: Why?

BELINDA: I work here. *(She closes the door.)* I made that bed. So don't pee in it or anything.

EVE: The sheets were very tight.

BELINDA: What's the matter with you? You naked under there?

EVE: No. What do you want?

BELINDA: Oh, nothing really. I'm just bored. *(She sits down at the end of the bed.)* I always get this way after some sex, a large pizza and the second box of wine. It gets boring.

EVE: Why don't you go home?

BELINDA: Now if that dump wasn't the most boring place on earth, you think I'd be hanging around here, the *second* most boring place on earth? This flea hole? Jesus.

EVE: I guess—

BELINDA: I'd love to watch my house burn to the ground...I'd dance around the fucking flames. I would. I just stand there and watch that same table, that same damn couch, that same goddamn wallpaper turn to fucking ashes. I picked that shit out too, and I still can't stand to look at it anymore.

EVE: Take it down—

BELINDA: Goddamn fruit, everywhere you look.
Fucking fruit. Apples, pears, bananas. I don't know
what I was thinking. I don't even like to eat the shit,
why would I want to stare at it day after day? Like
living in fucking bottle of Hawaiian Punch. *(She lies
down.)* God, what I'd give for a Carnival Cruise.
(She lies on her side.) Some ronde-fucking-vu. My
husband is snoring his fucking brains out in there.
I could be at home for this, at least have a book to
read or People magazine. Something.

EVE: You don't look old enough to be married.

BELINDA: How old do you have to look to be married?
A hundred?

EVE: I don't know. Eighteen—

BELINDA: I'm twenty. It's that old enough for you?
What happened to your eye?

EVE: Oh nothing...I fell.

BELINDA: How old are you?

EVE: Thirty-two.

BELINDA: No way.

(EVE laughs.)

EVE: Why would I lie about being thirty-two?

BELINDA: What are you doing here?

EVE: Just going—

BELINDA: You must use Oil of Olay.

EVE: What?

BELINDA: That's it. I swear, they don't lie with those
commercials. "You *can* look younger too." How many
kids you got?

EVE: Me? None.

BELINDA: What's the matter? You sterile?

EVE: No, I just haven't—

BELINDA: I've got two. Boys. Brats, both of them.
I really don't like kids much.

EVE: Why'd you have them?

BELINDA: Why's a dog have kids? Some stud sniffs
it out, catches it, mounts it and that's what happens.
Nature's fastest mistake. Just happened to happen to
me, twice. I have my tubes tied now. Lot less hassle.

EVE: I guess so.

BELINDA: But the boredom...shit...I wonder if I should
have kept them untied just to kill the boredom. Kids
do kinda shake things around the house, you know?

EVE: Uh huh.

BELINDA: Gives you something to talk about besides
dinner.

EVE: So you come sleep here for excitement?

BELINDA: Yeah. Yippee.

EVE: You know George?

BELINDA: George Banks?

EVE: Uh, yeah, Banks—

BELINDA: He went to school with my sister. He works at
the Chevron. Why?

EVE: I don't know...I just met him— (She laughs.)

BELINDA: You like him?

EVE: I just met him—

BELINDA: Weirdo.

EVE: Really?

BELINDA: Freak.

EVE: Why do you say that?

BELINDA: Just what he is. Everybody knows it. I never talk to him. I'd rather talk to my foot.

EVE: Really?

BELINDA: I heard he was born with a twin. And he killed it.

EVE: What?

BELINDA: People say he smothered him when he was three. Some kind of accident. He's a freak.

(EVE *moves away from* BELINDA. *Laughs*)

EVE: Won't your husband wonder where you are?

BELINDA: Yes.

EVE: Won't he worry?

BELINDA: That's the excitement. *(She slowly stands up.)* And he'll yell for awhile and then I'll cry and then... we're in love again. Fucking Valentines for ten whole goddamn minutes. *(She opens the door.)* You should put the chain on this. You never know who can sneak through. Weirdos all over this fucking place. *(She turns off the light and exits.)*

(EVE, *naked, gets out of bed and puts the chain on the door.*)

(EVE *approaches the mirror and can see more bruises on her body in the dim light. Marks on her ribs. Her thighs. Her shoulder*)

(LILY *rushes on with a wagon full of stuff. She pushes herself in front of* EVE *as she stares at herself in the mirror.*)

(LILY *quickly pulls lipstick, eye shadow, blush from the wagon and puts it on.*)

(LILY *touches one of* EVE's *bruises out of curiosity before she rushes off with the wagon in tow.*)

Scene Seven

(EVE *turns on the light.* LILY *is gone.*)

(*The bruises are black and blue on* EVE's *pale skin.*)

(EVE *puts on her pants and shirt. Removes an empty pill bottle from her bag, and unhooks the chain and unlocks the door.*)

(GEORGE *sits outside the door smoking.*)

GEORGE: Took you long enough.

EVE: Long enough for what?

GEORGE: To come outside.

EVE: I need to make a phone call.

GEORGE: You fell asleep.

EVE: I was tired.

GEORGE: It's too hot in your room, that's why. Who are you calling?

EVE: I met Belinda.

GEORGE: Oh yeah?

EVE: You just missed her.

GEORGE: No I didn't. She kissed me on her way out.

EVE: Nice local girl. Too bad she's taken, you could ask her to marry you.

GEORGE: She's not my type.

EVE: Why not?

GEORGE: She talks too much.

EVE: She had stories about you.

GEORGE: Did you believe them?

EVE: I haven't decided.

(EVE *laughs, keeps walking to a pay phone.* GEORGE *jumps up and follows.*)

GEORGE: Your eye looks worse.

(EVE *picks up the phone. Fishes a handful of change from her pocket. Begins to load it into the phone coin by coin.*)

GEORGE: It's probably the heat...I fucking hate August. It's not good for anything but money. It's always too hot. The end of the summer. Thirty-one days that feel like—

(EVE *puts one coin back in her pocket and studies the label on the pill bottle and dials a number.*)

GEORGE: What area code was that?

EVE: We always moved in August. *(Into the telephone)* San Francisco?

GEORGE: Calling home, huh?

EVE: Strange faces. A new school, the new girl— *(Into the telephone)* Longs Pharmacy please...yes, thanks...

GEORGE: Everybody wants to meet the new girl—

EVE: *(Into telephone)* Eve Webster?

GEORGE: Webster, huh?

EVE: *(Into telephone)* Pardon? No, I have a prescription—

GEORGE: We had a new girl at our school once. Tenth grade. She moved a year later. Suzanne something. A very shy girl.

EVE: The new girl is usually shy. *(Into telephone)* Can you charge my— No? Oh? How much? I thought that was paid—oh. No, that's O K. Thank you. *(She hangs up the phone.)*

GEORGE: I talked to her once. Her bra strap was showing and I told her.... Who was that?

EVE: You wanna have sex?

Scene Eight

(Eve quickly sits up. Naked. Sweaty. Away from GEORGE *on the edge of the bed.)*

EVE: Nothing.

GEORGE: Did I hurt you?

EVE: No.

*(*GEORGE *rubs the bruise on* EVE's *shoulder.)*

GEORGE: You really hit the ground hard, huh?

EVE: It was dark.

GEORGE: Are you sure I didn't hurt you?

EVE: Yes... *(She laughs, grabs the bible from the drawer. Opens the book at random.)* "In quietness and in confidence shall be your strength."

GEORGE: Eve?

*(*EVE *puts the bible back in the drawer.)*

GEORGE: I guess there are some words of wisdom in that book.

EVE: The dictionary beats it.

GEORGE: If you *use* the words.

*(*EVE *lies back on the bed.)*

GEORGE: Your quiet is killing my confidence.

EVE: I haven't been touched like that. In a long time.

GEORGE: Was it wrong?

EVE: No.

GEORGE: Then why are you afraid of me now?

(GEORGE *reaches for her again.* EVE *pulls away.*)

EVE: It was tender. I wasn't expecting it. (*She gets out of bed and heads for the mirror.*) I dated a Japanese man and we spoke through a dictionary for the first four months...

GEORGE: The one that kissed your foot?

EVE: I understood him better than I've ever understood anyone. (*She inspects herself.*)

GEORGE: What happened to him?

EVE: He's married. Three kids. Did you kill your brother?

GEORGE: No. Why didn't he marry you?

EVE: I wasn't ready. We met in China and then when we went to Japan, it was different. Belinda said you smothered him.

GEORGE: She lies. What happened in Japan?

EVE: We were in a restaurant, I leaned into to kiss him...and he backed away. Why would she lie about that?

GEORGE: She's bored. What do you mean he backed away?

(EVE *walks over, bends down to kiss* GEORGE. *He leans forward to match her lips and she pulls away.*)

EVE: He said that in Japan, it was custom to respect the people around you. To not disturb them with affection... All those things I thought didn't really matter...did. Did you have a brother?

GEORGE: Yes. You may have done the same thing.

EVE: Where? What happened to him?

GEORGE: He died.... Why are you...you got a thing for killers? In the United States.

EVE: We don't have any customs. How'd he die?

GEORGE: He stopped breathing. We have a few—

EVE: I couldn't have survived Japan anyway...I would rather rot alone in America than play geisha girl. Did you help him?

GEORGE: No. No one wants to rot alone. Besides, the costume's pretty cool.

EVE: I suppose. If you enjoy costumes. Did you watch him? (*She dresses.*)

GEORGE: Yes. America has customs.

EVE: Name them. Will you tell me about it?

GEORGE: Never. Grace before dinner. Toasting at weddings. Wiping your feet before you enter a house. Shaking hands. The good-night kiss on the first date. Valentine's Day. Christmas lights. No shirts no shoes no service.

EVE: All of which are broken every day. When was the last time you said Grace at dinner?

GEORGE: Last night.

EVE: With your parents?

GEORGE: "Be present at our table Lord, be here and everywhere adored, these mercies bless and grant that we, may feast and fellowship with thee. Amen." Yes.

EVE: Do you eat with them often?

GEORGE: Uh huh. We say Grace every time. They are firm believers in that book.

EVE: What do you believe in?

GEORGE: Changing your oil every three thousand miles.

EVE: Do you have your own place?

GEORGE: No.

EVE: Why not?

GEORGE: I don't need it.

EVE: Why not?

GEORGE: There's no place like home.

EVE: Same room?

GEORGE: Well, when we get married, I figure some things will have to change. I know a house. Down the road about six miles. It's just sitting there. Waiting.

EVE: Waiting?

GEORGE: Yeah.

EVE: Maybe you should move into it. Then you don't have to wait.

GEORGE: I don't want to live alone.

EVE: You can learn a lot about yourself that way.

GEORGE: I've heard that.

EVE: It's true.

GEORGE: What have you learned?

(EVE *puts on her shoes.*)

EVE: The suns about to come up and I should get going.

GEORGE: Where?

EVE: What's it matter to you?

GEORGE: I like you.

(EVE *picks up* GEORGE'*s clothes.*)

EVE: Your pants.

GEORGE: Where are you going?

EVE: And your shoes.

GEORGE: You have no money—

EVE: That's my problem.

GEORGE: Stay. Here.

EVE: In this town?

GEORGE: Here would be this town.

EVE: I'd die in a place like this.

GEORGE: Seems like where you've been hasn't exactly been feeding you—

EVE: Are you going to get dressed?

GEORGE: I like you.

EVE: I heard you the first time.... Could you please put your pants on? I'm losing time.

GEORGE: For what?

EVE: And your shirt.

(GEORGE *dresses. Slips on his shoes*)

GEORGE: Not even a good-bye kiss?

(EVE *doesn't respond. She opens the door.*)

(GEORGE *holds out his hand to shake* EVE's.)

GEORGE: Grant me this one small American custom.

(EVE *shakes his hand.*)

(GEORGE *pulls* EVE's *hand to his cheek, holds it there.*)

(GEORGE *lets go.*)

GEORGE: Be careful of strangers. They don't know who you are. *(He exits.)*

(EVE *opens her hand to a hundred dollars.*)

END OF ACT ONE

ACT TWO

Scene One

(Inside the motel room. Morning)

(BELINDA enters with cleaning supplies. She's hungover and slow. She begins to strip the bed.)

(EVE exits from the bathroom in a towel.)

BELINDA: Check out's at noon, you know.

EVE: I know.

BELINDA: Are you one of those...one of those...what do you call them...nudist?

EVE: No.

BELINDA: How come you're always naked?

EVE: Because you never knock. *(She laughs.)*

BELINDA: Whatever.

EVE: It's still my room.

BELINDA: I thought you'd be gone.

EVE: I've got plenty of time—

BELINDA: Yeah, well, don't pussy-foot around. I've got a lot of rooms to clean. Damn 4-H club checked out this morning and left the place in a fucking pig sty. Freaks.

EVE: Why don't you go clean those rooms and let me take a shower?

BELINDA: I always start this side of the building.

EVE: Start on the other side.

(BELINDA *plops on the bed.*)

BELINDA: I feel like shit. I wish I could throw up.
I hate this job.

EVE: Look, I am trying to get out of here. If you'll let
me shower—

BELINDA: You do kind of smell.... Smells like sex.

EVE: I don't think so— *(She laughs.)*

BELINDA: Yep, that's what it is.

EVE: No—

BELINDA: I can sniff out every single thing that goes on
in this place. So don't tell me that's not sex. This nose is
a fucking ace detective. I walk into a room and I know.
Instantly. Perfume is a dead give away— Be careful,
Jovan musk is like a fucking bulls-eye— Aftershave.
Baby powder. Baby shit. Dogs. Cats. Ferrets. Booze.
Cheese curls. You name it. Things I wish I'd never
smelled.

EVE: You're wrong about this—

BELINDA: Look at the bed. Both sides are messy.
Did you do that yourself?

EVE: Yes.

BELINDA: Bullshit.

EVE: Restless night.

BELINDA: Uh huh.

EVE: I've got a long day ahead of me—

BELINDA: Should have got an early start then, huh?

EVE: I'm trying.

BELINDA: Doesn't look like it. Books open. Clothes are half packed. Shoes are over there. Bed's warm.

EVE: It's still early—

BELINDA: Too fucking early. Damn owner thinks we Americans like to work at the break of dawn. That shit might fly in Korea, but I'm in no hurry to get on my hands and knees to clean up semen stains and red neck vomit. *(She gets up.)* There's not enough Mr. Clean in the world for that shit. I swear I'm lucky I don't go fucking crazy from all the things I've seen in this place. You wouldn't believe...people don't give a flying fuck what they do outside their own homes. Who has to clean it up. Disgusting people traveling this country. Freaks. Animals most of them. *(She grabs her cleaning supplies.)* But, looks like your company was decent. Little beer, little food...nothing was broken. One night stand. Huh?

EVE: No.

BELINDA: Did he rough you up?

EVE: What?

BELINDA: All those bruises.

EVE: No—

BELINDA: Where'd you meet him?

EVE: I didn't have a one night—

BELINDA: I could use one of those. What's his name?

EVE: I don't know anyone here. How could I have a one night stand?

BELINDA: Easy. The men are so hard up this town all you have to do is spit at them and they'll come in their pants. *(She heads for the door.)* But looks like you already found that out. *(She picks up one of the beer bottles.)* It wasn't my husband was it?

EVE: He was with you.

BELINDA: Oh yeah...that's right. I guess I should go clean 29 first. Get that puke before it dries.

EVE: Uh huh.

BELINDA: I told him he had too much. He won't stop until the whole box is gone. Idiot. *(She sees the empty pill bottle and pen on the dresser on the way out. Picks up both. Studies the pill bottle first)* Hello. What are these?

EVE: They're gone.

BELINDA: What were they? Anything good?

EVE: No.

BELINDA: I could use a party. Something to blow my fucking mind right out of my head.

EVE: Those wouldn't do that.

BELINDA: What would they do?

EVE: Prevent it.

BELINDA: Prevent what?

EVE: Mind blowing— *(She throws down the bottle.)*

BELINDA: Hap's Chevron. You get a fill up there?

EVE: Uh. Yeah.

(BELINDA clicks the pen and looks around the room.)

BELINDA: Uh huh...looks like that's not all you got.

EVE: I got the pen. *(She laughs.)*

BELINDA: And a freak to go with it?

EVE: I'd like to take a shower.

BELINDA: Did he blow your mind?

EVE: I'd like to take a shower—

BELINDA: Well, well, well. Looks like there's a new girl on the block, huh?

EVE: No.

BELINDA: Rounding up the bad boys. *(She opens the door. I better be careful.*

(BELINDA *throws the pen to* EVE.*)*

BELINDA: You could be the talk of the town. *(She exits.)*

(EVE *locks the door. Surveys the room. She sits on the bed. Then sees her Walkman on the floor by her bag. She picks up the headphones, puts them on. Turns over a tape in the Walkman. Pushes the play button. She returns to the bed, rubbing her forehead.)*

(The Velvet Underground's Some Kinda Love plays.)

(EVE *sits moving her head to the music.)*

(LILY *enters the stage in her mother's shoes. She's carrying a stack of her own records in one hand, and a box of toys in the other. Looking for a place to put them)*

(LILY *can't help but begin to dance, around the room, around* EVE. *An odd misshapen sexual dance)*

(EVE *continues to move her head; sings to some of the lyrics.)*

(LILY *dances.)*

(GEORGE *stands outside the motel room door. His hands covered in grease.)*

(EVE *stands and exits into the bathroom.)*

(LILY *continues to dance. She opens the motel room door. She strains to be taller. She stands on the box. She kisses* GEORGE *and closes the door behind her. She's searching as she exits.)*

(GEORGE *moves closer to the door. Touching his lips)*

Scene Two

(GEORGE *stands with his ear against the door.*)

(*Inside the room,* EVE *walks out of the bathroom, wet from the shower. She checks herself out in the mirror, then heads for door.*)

(*Listens*)

(EVE *puts her ear up against the door.*)

(GEORGE *puts his hand up against the wood, his whole body against the door.*)

(EVE *does the same.*)

(*Listen*)

(*Both slowly walk away from the door, disappointed with the silence on the other side.*)

Scene Three

(EVE *paces, holding the $100 bill in one hand and clicking the pen in the other. Her bags are packed by the door. She sits on the bed. Stands. Looks in the mirror. Sits on the bed. Turns on the T V. She shuts off the television. She puts the money in her back pocket.*)

Scene Four

(EVE *stands at the pay phone just outside her room. The pen still in her hand.*)

EVE: (*Into phone*) It's Eve...I want to come see you....
Can you hear me? ...There's, there's a pause between
what you say and—you can? ...O K...yeah... Sorry to call

you collect but— ...no, I've, I've got enough money.
I'm fine. Listen, I was thinking maybe I could come
over there and see you—I said, I want to come see—
...I'm, I'm in Idaho...I drove here— ...I don't know the
name of the town— ...of course I'm looking for work...
no...I'm looking for a job...not here but— ...Uh huh...
Well, I'll take anything at this point—....I know...but
a college degree doesn't guarantee much— ...I have to
start somewhere, don't I? ...I wasn't fired from that job.
I quit— ...I'm not a quitter— ...Because I don't want to
be a secretary— ...I know he was your friend. But he
was a terrible— ...Have you talked to Mom?...Mom?
Dad? ...Can you hear me— ...I think you should call
her—...it is too my business.

(The MANAGER *and* DEAN *enter carrying coffee and
doughnuts.)*

MANAGER: I don't like loose girls in my rooms. It's no
good for business.

DEAN: She's not a prostitute, Dad. I already asked her.

MANAGER: Check-out's at noon. No hanky panky in my
motel.

EVE: *(Into phone)* It's is too. You want to leave, break
us all apart but you don't want anyone to argue or talk
about it...jesus...we're your family—Dad?

MANAGER: You stay you pay. But no sex.

EVE: *(Into phone)* What? ...Well, can't the meeting wait?
...Tell the Koreans to wait— ...Dad?

MANAGER: Weekend's coming. We get booked up.
I want good people, no crazy girls. O K?

EVE: *(Into phone)* I'm having seizures.

DEAN: You talking to Korea? Can I talk?

*(*EVE *puts down the phone.)*

MANAGER: Don't be silly.

DEAN: What did he say?

(EVE *searches her pockets for change. She only has a quarter.*)

EVE: Damn it.

DEAN: How's the weather?

EVE: Can I borrow ten cents?

MANAGER: Shut up. You're not going to Korea.

DEAN: I am. (*He finds a dime in his pockets.*) Here.

EVE: Thanks.

MANAGER: Go fix that toilet in 40.

DEAN: Here.

(DEAN *hands* EVE *a cup of coffee.*)

EVE: Thanks.

DEAN: It's my home.

MANAGER: This is your home. Now go.

DEAN: I hate it here.

(*The* MANAGER *pops* DEAN *on the head.*)

(DEAN *hands* EVE *a doughnut.*)

DEAN: Here.

EVE: Thanks—

DEAN: America sucks. (*He quickly exits.*)

(EVE *studies the number on the pen. Puts the change in the phone*)

MANAGER: You stay another night?

(EVE *dials the number. She feels a seizure coming on.*)

MANAGER: I don't like funny business in my motel.

(EVE *hangs up.*)

EVE: Excuse me, I don't feel very well.

MANAGER: No party girls here.

EVE: I don't feel—

MANAGER: I mean it.

EVE: Please—

(EVE *closes the door in the* MANAGER'*s face.*)

MANAGER: Twelve o'clock. On the dot. Or you pay.

(EVE *drops the coffee and doughnut, falls to the floor into another seizure.*)

(*Slides of* EVE *with her family flash against the stage: Mom, Dad,* EVE'*s older sister, and* EVE *[as* LILY*] in shots of various years growing up—Christmas, beach vacations, camping, skiing, laughing in the kitchen, playing with dogs in the yard, laying in bed, sleeping, etc.*)

(LILY *enters, walking backwards. A pile of toys in her hand. Looking at something in the distance. Her dress is dirty. Her arms are scratched. One knee is bleeding. An old band-aid is on the other knee.*)

LILY: You can have her!

(LILY *backs up and trips over* EVE. *Toys scatter everywhere.* EVE *comes to.*)

(LILY *stands up. Continues shouting at the distance*)

LILY: I didn't want her anyway! (*She throws the Barbie in the distance.*)

EVE: Lily?

(LILY *picks up the rest of the toys she'd dropped. A doll. A stuffed animal, etc*)

EVE: Lily?

LILY: Damn it.

EVE: Lily.

LILY: What?

(EVE *tries to grab her. Look more closely at her.* LILY *squirms out of her grip.*)

LILY: I need a suitcase. Do you have a suitcase?

EVE: No—

LILY: Damn it.

EVE: You're bleeding.

LILY: So.

EVE: You're knee. You're arm—

LILY: I don't care. I— (*She drops all her things.*)

LILY: Damn it.

EVE: Where are you going—

LILY: Won't even buy me a suitcase. Jane got one.

(EVE *looks in the distance. Finally notices the slides around her.*)

EVE: Is Jane coming?

LILY: Who cares. (*She struggles to hold everything.*)

(EVE *picks up a doll.*)

EVE: I remember her—

(LILY *rips her from her hands.*)

LILY: She's mine.

EVE: Dad gave her to me.

LILY: She's mine.

EVE: Where are you going?

LILY: No where. I'm not going this time.

(EVE *picks a slide.*)

EVE: There?

LILY: Where?

EVE: There's me. In North Carolina—

LILY: Hold this.

(LILY *hands the handful of stuff to* EVE.)

EVE: Why?

LILY: I've got an itch. (*She rips off the band-aid and scratches her knee. Wipes the blood on her dress*) Damn it.

(LILY *looks at* EVE. *Sees the slides*)

LILY: Where am I?

EVE: With me.

LILY: Who?

EVE: You.

(LILY *takes her stuff back.*)

LILY: Do you have a suitcase?

EVE: Yes.

LILY: Can I have it?

EVE: No.

LILY: Why not?

EVE: I need it.

LILY: What for?

EVE: Me.

LILY: But look at all this stuff? Where am I going to put it?

EVE: I don't know—

LILY: Dad said there's no more room in the car.

EVE: Keep it—

LILY: My room is empty.

EVE: Which one?

LILY: They took my bed. My bike.

EVE: Which one?

LILY: The pink one.

EVE: I liked that one—

LILY: I don't even have my damn kick ball. They packed it.

EVE: Maybe Mom will buy you a new one—

LILY: I need a suitcase. *(She tries to hold all her things. She's getting frustrated. Every time she gets close to holding everything, something falls.)*

EVE: Let, let me help you—

(LILY starts to cry. Throws everything across the stage)

LILY: Damn it! Damn it! Damn it all to hell!

EVE: Wait—

(LILY kicks the things until they are fly off stage.)

EVE: What are you doing? Those are my things—

LILY: They're mine!

EVE: You like them.

LILY: Who cares?

EVE: I do.

LILY: Why? What are you going to do with them?

EVE: Save them. Keep them. Put them away for my—

LILY: Your what?

EVE: Family.

LILY: What family?

EVE: Mine. Someday I might want things—

LILY: Take mine.

EVE: What?

LILY: Family.

EVE: Why?

LILY: I hate them.

EVE: Why?

LILY: They won't stay still.

EVE: But they're fun. You don't want to give them away. Look. They look like fun.

(The slides change as they speak. Pieces of the images that they remember.)

LILY: Sometimes.

EVE: See there's—isn't that Dad?

LILY: He's older now.

EVE: I know, but there, there he's—

LILY: He can be fun. Sometimes.

EVE: See. He's spinning you around.

LILY: Only because he was getting ready to leave.

EVE: For where?

LILY: Vietnam.

EVE: I see—

LILY: And he didn't come back for two years.

EVE: We heard his voice on a tape recorder.

LILY: Uh huh.

EVE: I remember he smelled like—

LILY: Grass.

EVE: Brut.

LILY: Blood.

EVE: He listened to Vietnamese music.

LILY: He was quiet.

EVE: We dressed up the dog.

LILY: In my clothes.

EVE: And then—

LILY: We moved again. Damn it. *(She pouts on the floor.)* I wish I had my bike. *(She picks at her knee.)*

EVE: Maryland was nice. Wasn't it—

LILY: I don't know.

EVE: We had a big room.

LILY: So.

EVE: It had wallpaper. Flowers—

LILY: So?

EVE: You picked it out—

LILY: I didn't get to stay in it.

EVE: Still—

(LILY lies on her back.)

LILY: I don't want move again. Damn it.

EVE: There are some great places. Virginia. Rhode Island. Norway—

LILY: I've never been there.

EVE: I promise you, you will like—

LILY: I'm tired of promises. No one ever keeps them.

EVE: You can.

LILY: Why bother.

EVE: Mom keeps them—

LILY: So.

EVE: She's good at them.

LILY: Can you shut up?

EVE: What?

(LILY sits up.)

LILY: You talk too much. *(She looks around.)* How do I get out of here?

EVE: Where?

LILY: Here.

EVE: Why?

LILY: I want to get out.

EVE: Why?

LILY: I'm hungry.

EVE: Maybe I can find you—I'll find you food—

LILY: I want my own house.

EVE: What for? Maybe you can live here—

LILY: I can paint ducks on the wall. Sea gulls. Pigeons if I want.

EVE: But you'd be alone.

LILY: I wouldn't need a suitcase.

EVE: You'd be lonely.

LILY: No.

EVE: You might.

LILY: What do you know?

EVE: A few things—

LILY: I don't need a few things. I need a car.

EVE: What for?

LILY: To put in my garage. Let it rust. Let rats live in it.

EVE: But you love riding in the car—

LILY: My friends can come and feed them cheese—

EVE: You like singing with Jane. Mom and Dad. You get to eat at McDonalds. Stay in motels. Swim in the pools. See—

LILY: It's alright.

EVE: You'd miss riding with them.

LILY: I don't want to ride with them.

EVE: All together—

LILY: I want to eat dinner together. At home.

EVE: You do that—

LILY: Sometimes.

EVE: And you get to have breakfast in bed—

LILY: Where's my bed now?

EVE: Well—

LILY: You don't know anything, do you?

EVE: I do—

LILY: Then how do I get out of here?

EVE: Lily—

LILY: How do I get out? *(She begins to search an exit.)*

EVE: Lily please don't go—

LILY: Let me out. *(She runs around the room. Panicked. She can't find a way out now.)* Get me out!

EVE: You can stay—

LILY: I don't want to. I want Mom.

EVE: Lily—

LILY: Daddy?

EVE: Lily—

LILY: Jane? Come get me! Come get me!

EVE: Please no. Stay here. With me—

LILY: Come get me! Will somebody come get me!

EVE: You can stay—

LILY: I want to come home!

EVE: I won't hurt you—

LILY: I want to go home! Somebody come get me!
(She can't find a way out.) SOMEBODY! *(She turns on
EVE.)* Tell them to come get me.

EVE: They won't.

(LILY sits on the floor. Curls up)

(EVE walks over to her.)

LILY: They don't love me.

EVE: They do.

LILY: But I'm tired. Can't they come get me?

EVE: I don't think so.

LILY: They don't love me.

EVE: No. They do. I know they do.

LILY: Where are they?

EVE: They're driving.

LILY: Where? Without me?

EVE: They're going other places.

LILY: Without me?

EVE: Yes.

LILY: Why?

EVE: I guess they have to.

LILY: Where will I sleep?

EVE: Here.

LILY: It stinks. It's smells like strangers. I want to go home.

EVE: You can't go there.

LILY: Why not?

EVE: It's gone.

(LILY is devastated.)

LILY: No...

(EVE picks LILY up and carries her to the bed. LILY struggles.)

LILY: I want to sleep in my own bed.

EVE: You can sleep here.

LILY: It's too scary.

EVE: I'll be here.

LILY: I want my house.

EVE: You can sleep with me.

(EVE places LILY on the bed.)

EVE: I'll put the car in the garage.

(LILY stops struggling.)

EVE: I'll paint birds on the walls.

LILY: What kind?

EVE: Pigeons.

LILY: Ducks?

EVE: In a row.

(LILY sits up.)

LILY: Sea gulls?

EVE: Flying to the ceiling. Out the window.

LILY: Can I sleep as late as I want?

EVE: All day.

LILY: Can I eat all the food in the world?

EVE: Til you're full—

(LILY looks EVE over.)

EVE: Stuffed.

LILY: Let me smell you first.

EVE: What?

(LILY smells her neck.)

LILY: Let me touch your face. *(She touches EVE's face.)* Let me see your hands.

(LILY puts her hands palm to palm with EVE.)

LILY: Let me see your eyes.

(LILY looks EVE eye to eye.)

LILY: Who are you?

EVE: Eve.

(LILY lies down beside EVE.)

LILY: You'll do.

Scene Five

(EVE is curled up on the bed. She comes to. Slowly)

(EVE stands and looks around the room. LILY is gone.)

(Still unsteady, EVE grabs her bag. She leans against the door and cries.)

(EVE finally stops herself, wipes her eyes, and opens the door.)

(GEORGE *is standing outside. He steps face to face with* EVE.)

GEORGE: Couldn't leave me, huh?

(EVE *steps back.*)

EVE: What?

GEORGE: Leave me.

(GEORGE *offers a handkerchief from his pocket.* EVE *refuses it.*)

EVE: I had things to do.

GEORGE: Like what?

(EVE *takes the money from her pocket.*)

GEORGE: You're welcome.

EVE: I don't want it.

GEORGE: I don't want it back. You shouldn't have stuck around for that.

EVE: I didn't.

GEORGE: Stay for the free breakfast? (*He kicks the doughnut.*)

EVE: Shouldn't you be at work.

GEORGE: Were you planning to stop by?

EVE: No.

GEORGE: Good. You would have missed me—

EVE: I wouldn't miss you—

GEORGE: It's my lunch break.

EVE: What time is it?

GEORGE: Want to join me?

EVE: What time is it?

GEORGE: Twelve O three.

EVE: Shit. Move.

GEORGE: What's the hurry?

EVE: I need to check out.

GEORGE: Stay awhile.

EVE: I can't.

GEORGE: Why not?

EVE: I have to check out.

GEORGE: I hear they're pretty strict with that here.

EVE: Move.

GEORGE: Do they make you pay for another night?

EVE: Move.

GEORGE: I mean, if they make you pay for it, your room, a place to stay, you wouldn't just leave it behind.

EVE: I might.

(GEORGE *moves in closer.*)

GEORGE: Really?

EVE: Yes.

GEORGE: Why?

EVE: I don't know.

(GEORGE *tries to touch* EVE's *face.*)

EVE: George...

GEORGE: Yes?

EVE: Please move.

GEORGE: I don't want to.

EVE: Please.

GEORGE: I don't want to.

EVE: Move.

(GEORGE *moves in close enough to kiss* EVE. *They could*—)

EVE: Please?

(GEORGE *steps back.*)

(EVE *moves towards* GEORGE, *puts the money in his shirt pocket, and exits.*)

(GEORGE *watches* EVE *go, then enters the room.*)

(GEORGE *looks at the bed, begins to wander the room, touching the things that* EVE *has touched. The beer bottles. The sandwich. He picks up the empty pill bottle. Studies it. Puts it in his pocket. He quickly passes the mirror without looking. He picks up the Bible. Opens it)*

GEORGE: Amen. (*Puts it down*)

(GEORGE *picks up* EVE's *pillow and smells it.*)

(BELINDA *enters.*)

BELINDA: What are you doing?

GEORGE: Dreaming.

BELINDA: Well, do it someplace else. I gotta clean.

GEORGE: What if she comes back?

BELINDA: Hey. Freak. Do you mind? I'm not trying to make a career out of this.

GEORGE: I'm not stopping you. (*He walks around the room with the pillow.*) Am I?

BELINDA: Can't you find a tire to change? Lubricate something?

GEORGE: Nope.

BELINDA: Like anyone would come back for you.

GEORGE: What do you know?

BELINDA: Plenty.

GEORGE: You've never been anywhere. *(He is close to the mirror.)*

BELINDA: Get out. *(She pulls the pillow from GEORGE's hands.)* You're getting your fucking greasy hands on everything.

(GEORGE catches sight of his hands in the mirror. He leaves them there.)

GEORGE: Aren't they beautiful?

(EVE enters.)

EVE: What'd you do?

GEORGE: Huh? *(He is engrossed in the reflection of his hands.)*

EVE: My car. It won't start.

GEORGE: Really?

EVE: What did you do?

GEORGE: Huh?

EVE: To my car?

GEORGE: Your car?

EVE: It won't start.

GEORGE: Did you turn the key?

EVE: Don't fuck with me, George.

BELINDA: Sounds like you two already took care of that. Freaks. *(She exits into the bathroom.)*

GEORGE: Huh?

EVE: It won't move.

GEORGE: Oh.

EVE: George?

GEORGE: Yes...

EVE: What did you do?

GEORGE: Eve.

EVE: Look at me.

(EVE *realizes* GEORGE *is looking at his hands in the mirror.*)

EVE: George?

GEORGE: Here.

EVE: What, what did you do?

(EVE *slowly reaches. Their hands meet, then join.*)

(EVE *pulls him closer. She and* GEORGE *stand together, side-by-side, facing themselves in the mirror.*)

GEORGE: Aren't they beautiful?

END OF PLAY